Introduction

The oceans and seas are some of the most diverse habitats on Earth, and cover around three-quarters of our planet. They help to regulate Earth's climate, produce more than half of the oxygen in the atmosphere and absorb enormous amounts of carbon dioxide. The oceans are teeming with life, from microscopic single-celled plankton, to ferocious sharks and giant whales. These watery worlds contain some of the planet's most fascinating ecosystems.

Contents

Read on to **find** out more about **oceans** of the **world**...

The global ocean

Oceans cover about 70 per cent of the **Earth's** surface and they carry out many functions. Oceans affect the **weather** and **temperature** of our planet. They moderate Earth's temperature by absorbing heat from the **Sun**. The ocean's waves and **currents** distribute this heat energy around the world, heating the land and air during winter and **cooling** them during summer. There are five **oceans** on Earth and they are all connected to one another. **Seas** are smaller than oceans, but far more numerous. Most seas are bordered in part or **completely** by land.

Deepest point

The Mariana Trench in the Pacific Ocean is the deepest place on Earth. It is 11 kilometres in depth.

Salt and fresh water

Barely three per cent of water on Earth is fresh; 97.5 per cent is salty. Two per cent of fresh water is frozen in glaciers. The rest, in lakes and rivers, is drinking water.

A surfer riding a large wave off the coast of Hawaii

Did you know?

When Earth is photographed from space its looks mostly blue because of the amount of the water. This has lead scientists to nickname our planet, the 'blue marble'.

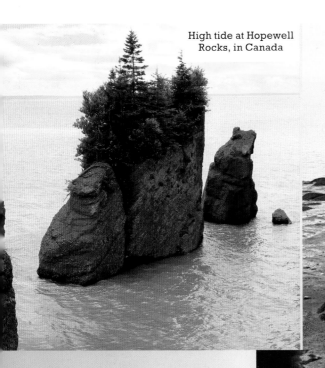

High tide at Hopewell Rocks, in Canada

Low tide at Hopewell Rocks, in Canada

Water levels

Every 12 hours or so, seawater rises and recedes. These movements are called tides. As Earth turns, the Moon 'pulls' the seawater towards itself, causing water to rise. High and low tides are most noticeable along coasts, where rocks and beaches are exposed and then submerged under water.

Ocean storms

Enormous tropical storms with powerful winds and heavy rain can develop over warm waters. These storms, called cyclones, can be hundreds of kilometres across. Cyclones also create tornadoes, high waves and widespread flooding when they hit land, causing devastation.

A cyclone near the coast of Florida

Some of the largest waves can be found around the Hawaiian Islands in the Pacific Ocean.

Ocean study

Scientists who study marine ecosystems, ocean circulation and geology are called oceanographers.

Salty water

As rainwater flows over and under land on its way to the sea, it collects mineral salts. As sea water evaporates, the saltiness increases.

Ships on the Strait of Malacca, Malaysia

Ocean highways

As the modern world developed, many countries began trading goods with each other. Soon sea routes were established and ships began carrying goods from continent to continent. Hundreds of years later we still use the oceans to transport commodities, foods and fuels around the world.

Down through the zones

An ocean can be divided into layers or **zones**. Each zone is defined by the amount of **sunlight** it receives, its depth and its level of water **pressure**. The top zone, called the sunlight zone, receives most sunlight and it is here that **aquatic** plants are able to grow. As you travel **down** through the twilight zone and into the midnight zone it becomes colder and **darker**, oxygen levels are reduced and pressure increases with the **weight** of the water above. Some sea **creatures** live their whole lives in a single zone, while others have to move **between** zones in order to survive.

Facts and figures

Oceanic zones

Sunlight zone
Surface – 200 metres
This zone gets lots of light and the Sun warms the water. Animal and plant life are plentiful.

Twilight zone
200 – 1,000 metres
Little light reaches this zone, so the water is cooler. Water pressure is increasing. Creatures that produce light start to appear in this zone.

Midnight zone
1,000 – 4,000 metres
Animals that live in this cold, dark zone are often black or red in colour due to lack of sunlight.

The Abyss
4,000 – 6,000 metres
There is no light and it is near freezing.

The Trenches
6,000 – 11,000 metres
Almost freezing water, and with water pressure equal to the weight of eight 747 aircraft.

Did you know?

The lanternfish is bioluminescent, producing light by a chemical reaction in its photophores. At night it migrates from the twilight zone to the surface to feed on plankton.

Almost unknown

Humans have only explored around five per cent of the oceans. In fact, we have better maps of Mars than of the ocean floor!

Undersea mountains

The mid-ocean ridges make up Earth's longest mountain range. It is 65,000 kilometres long and 90 per cent of it is underwater. It circles the globe like the seam on a tennis ball.

Teams of dolphins herd sardines into a densely packed shoal near the surface of the water

Over 90 per cent of all marine life lives in the sunlight zone.

Visual Explorers

Ocean Life

Published in 2019 by Franklin Watts,
Carmelite House, 50 Victoria Embankment
London, EC4Y 0DZ, United Kingdom

Created and produced by:
Green Android Ltd
49 Beaumont Court
Upper Clapton Road
London E5 8BG
United Kingdom

MIX
Paper from
responsible sources
FSC® C104723

ISBN 978-1-4451-6817-3

Printed and bound in Dongguan, China, June 2019

Franklin Watts is a division of Hachette Children's Books
An Hachette UK company
www.hachette.co.uk

Photo credits:
Images © www.flpa-images.co.uk: laternfish, purple sea urchin © Norbert Wu/Minden Pictures/FLPA. Images © www.shutterstock.com:
coral reef p14 © Richard Whitcombe; puffins © Spumador; frenzy of sharks © A Cotton Photo; humpback whales © Achimdiver;
lobe-finned fish © AlessandroZocc; anemonefish © Andaman; malacca straits © anekoho; chinstrap penguins © Anton_Ivanov;
coral polyp © aquapix; black skimmer © Arto Hakola, rookpool © blueeyes; triggerfish © bluehand; blue footed boobies © BlueOrange
Studio; pelican diving © Brian Florky; muddy coast © BW Folsom; pelican © Catcher of Light, Inc; gannet © Charles Masters; strawberry
anemones © Chelsea Cameron; wandering albatross © Christian Wilkinson; common lobster © davidpstephens; krill © digitalbalance;
red sea fan © DJ Mattaar; antarctic krill © Dmytro Pylypenko; black tip shark © Dray van Beeck; whale shark © Dudarev Mikhail; jellyfish
p32 © easyshutter; great white shark © Elsa Hoffmann; surfer, garibaldi © EpicStockMedia; sea nettle jellyfish, kelp air bladder, table
coral, barrel sponge p16, stonefish © Ethan Daniels; anchovies, leopard shark © evantravels; cleaning shrimp © Fiona Ayerst; caribbean
reef shark © frantisekhojdysz; sea lions © George Burba; high tide © GVictoria; cyclone over florida © Harvepino; manta ray © haveseen;
polar bear diving © Henrik Winther Andersen; angelfish © Irina Afonskaya; adelie penguin © Jan Martin Will; horseshoe crabs © Jana
Shea; humpback with open mouth © John Tunney; penguin diving © Josh Anon; blue marlin © Joshua Francis; peacock mantis shrimp
© Jung Hsuan; cod fish © Krasowit; mackerel © Kristina Vackova; dolphins © Krzysztof Odziomek; egyptian seastar © LauraD; clownfish
p.1 © Levent Konuk; barnacle © Lia Caldas; earth © MarcelClemens; hammerhead © Mark Doherty; tiger sharks © Matt9122; low tide
© Melissa King; red rock crab © Michael Zysman; purple tube sponges © michelle peters; herring gull © nevenm; gannet colony ©
nickichen; sandy beach © NOBUHIRO ASADA; tube sponge © Ocean Image Photography; sea cucumber © orlandin; walrus, humpback
breaching © outdoorsman; rocky coast © Patryk Kosmider; batfish with sea slater © Paul Vinten; gooseneck barnacle © Paul Yates;
starfish eating sea urchin © Peter Leahy; feather star © R Gombarik; octopus © Rich Carey; orcas © Riegsecker; pacific sea nettle
jellyfish © S-F; blue sea squirt © scubaluna; batwing coral crab © Sean Lema; giant clam © Sebastien Burel; great white shark ©
Sergey Uryadnikov; sperm whale © Shane Gross; sea lion underwater © Shin Okamoto; mandarin fish © stockpix4u; crown-of-thorns
© think4photop; mouth of sea urchin, red cushion starfish © Vilainecrevette; lionfish © Vlad61; bull sharks © Willyam Bradberry;
sea otter © worldswildlifewonders; king penguin © Yongyut Kumsri. Images © www.istockphoto.com: sand dollars © mardog38; starfish
feet © 4kodiak; snow sign © bofotolux; sand tiger shark © StevenBenjamin. Images © National Oceanic and Atmospheric Administration
(www.noaa.gov): black smoker © OAR/National Undersea Research Program (NURP); Dumbo Octopus © NOAA Okeanos Explorer Program;
giant isopod © Expedition to the Deep Slope 2006, NOAA-OE; crossota © Hidden Ocean 2005 Expedition: NOAA Office of Ocean
Exploration; squid larva © Matt Wilson/Jay Clark, NOAA NMFS AFSC; diatoms © NSF Polar Programs; whale blowing © NOAA;
glass sponges © NOAA Okeanos Explorer Program, Gulf of Mexico 2012 Expedition.

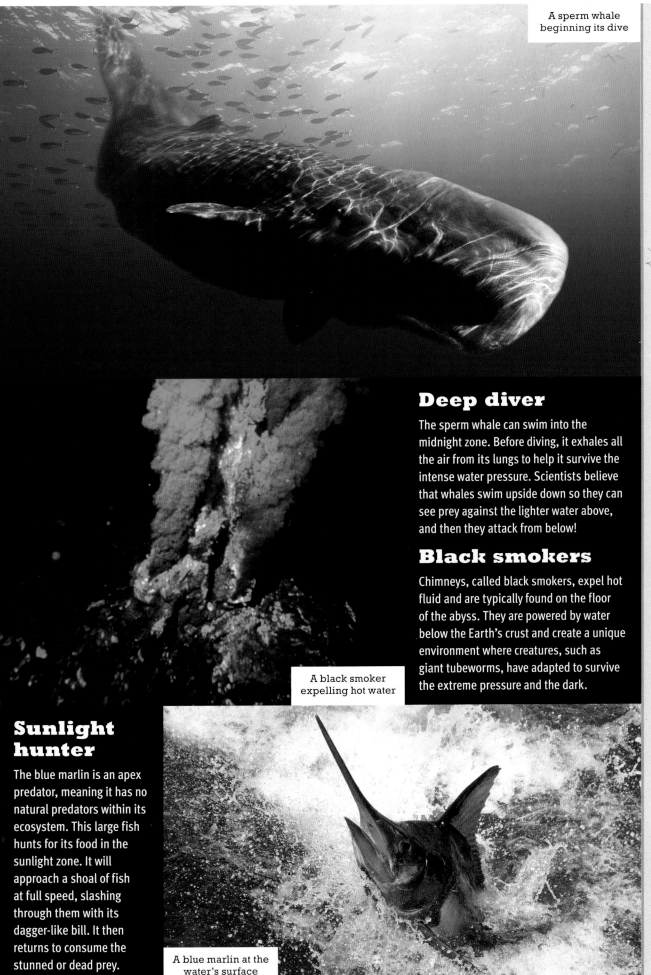

A sperm whale beginning its dive

A black smoker expelling hot water

A blue marlin at the water's surface

Deep diver

The sperm whale can swim into the midnight zone. Before diving, it exhales all the air from its lungs to help it survive the intense water pressure. Scientists believe that whales swim upside down so they can see prey against the lighter water above, and then they attack from below!

Black smokers

Chimneys, called black smokers, expel hot fluid and are typically found on the floor of the abyss. They are powered by water below the Earth's crust and create a unique environment where creatures, such as giant tubeworms, have adapted to survive the extreme pressure and the dark.

Sunlight hunter

The blue marlin is an apex predator, meaning it has no natural predators within its ecosystem. This large fish hunts for its food in the sunlight zone. It will approach a shoal of fish at full speed, slashing through them with its dagger-like bill. It then returns to consume the stunned or dead prey.

Marine food chains

Each **ecosystem** has its own food chain that shows the feeding connections between **species**. On the lowest level of the chain are **plankton**, which includes phytoplankton and zooplankton. The next level contains the **herbivores** who eat the phytoplankton and incorporate this energy into their own **tissues**. The **highest** levels contain animals – some that are microscopic, some that are ocean giants and apex **predators** – which eat other **organisms** for energy. If a link in the food chain breaks, it **threatens** the survival of all organisms in the chain.

Facts and figures

The food chain

The Sun
The Sun provides the energy for a food chain.

The producers
They use the Sun's energy to make food to store in their tissues.

The consumers
Consumers cannot make their own energy, but get it by eating the producers or consumers below them in the food chain. There are five levels of consumers.

Herbivore consumers
The lowest consumers, like krill and mussels, eat the producers.

Level 1 consumers
These carnivores eat herbivore consumers.

Levels 2 – 3 consumers
Larger carnivorous animals eat 1st and 2nd level consumers.

Levels 4 – 5 consumers
These consumers, such as sharks and whales, have no predators.

Mackerel eat small crustaceans and fish. They are eaten by larger animals including tuna, sharks and pelicans.

Did you know?

A pelican catches its food by scooping fish into its pouched bill. It squeezes the water from the pouch, tilts back its head and swallows the fish whole.

Threat of overfishing

A great threat to the marine food chain is overfishing by humans. Taking too many fish from a habitat can destroy the physical environment and distort the entire food chain.

Sea garden

Seaweeds are algae and are producers in the food chain. They need seawater, sunlight and an attachment point in order to grow.

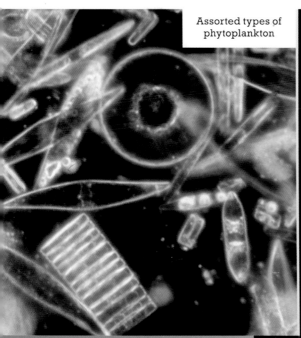
Assorted types of phytoplankton

Octopus larvae are a type of zooplankton

Micro organism

Plankton is the most basic organism in the ocean and is crucial in the food chain. There are two types of plankton: microscopic plants – called phytoplankton, and weak-swimming tiny animals – called zooplankton. Some zooplankton is made of baby animals that will grow into strong-swimming, non-planktonic adults.

Drifting jellyfish

Jellyfish primarily eat plankton, but larger specimens will also eat small crustaceans and fish. Some species are cannibalistic and will feed on other jellyfish. They use their stinging tentacles to catch their prey. Many species of sea turtle feed on jellyfish.

A group of Pacific sea nettle jellyfish

Flying predators

Sea birds, such as albatross, eat aquatic animals so they have an important role in the food chain.

Endless chain

Decomposers, such as marine worms, break down organic waste and dead plants and animals. These nutrients then re-enter the food chain.

Rising ocean temperatures are reducing phytoplankton numbers by one per cent every year.

Top predator

The great white shark is at the top of the marine food chain. It uses five senses – smell, taste, touch, sight and hearing – to capture prey, but is also able to sense electric fields through its pores. The shark uses this to navigate the oceans following a map of Earth's magnetic fields.

A great white shark catching a seal

Coastal life

Coastlines are areas where land meets an **ocean** or another large body of water. These areas are full of life, with plants, **algae**, flowers, **fish**, crustaceans, aquatic mammals and insects all making their homes here. **Rockpools** are formed at low tide. They provide **shelter** for many creatures that live below the waves. Clifftops along coastal areas are important **nesting** places for many **seabirds**. Coastal habitats also serve a vital function in the marine food chain and wider **environment**, providing feeding, **spawning** and nursery areas for many species.

Facts and figures

Grey seal record
The largest colony of grey seals is found on Sable Island, off Canada, where 100,000 come to breed in winter.

Gannets everywhere!
Bird Island, off the coast of South Africa, is home to 160,000 pairs of breeding gannets.

Long and short
Canada has the longest coastline – 244,781 kilometres. Monaco's is just 5.6 kilometres.

Disappearing fast
The Holderness Coast in England is eroding by two metres every year.

Going up!
Sweden's High Coast, which was weighed down by a glacier, is rising faster than any where else in the world.

Disappearing islands
It is believed that the islands of Kiribati in the middle of the Pacific Ocean will be under water by 2034.

Did you know?

Man-made harbours and ports are classed as areas of coastline. A large group of sea lions has relocated from rocky islands outside San Francisco Bay to wooden piers inside the bay.

Low tide along the coastline of Washington, USA.

Coral sand

Parrotfish eat coral, which is broken down and emerges from them as grains of sand. A parrotfish can produce 100 kilograms of beautiful, fine, white coral beach sand a year!

Working together

Colourful lichens often cover the rocks on coastlines. They are created when a fungi and algae grow together.

The rapidly changing conditions of a rockpool make survival a challenge.

A large cluster of blue mussels

Blue mussels are bivalve molluscs. This means they are simple animals with a soft body, protected by a hard shell that has two hinged parts. Mussels can be found on exposed shores, where they attach themselves with strong threads to rocks. They feed on plankton and other microscopic creatures.

Factfile

Types of coastline

Coastlines support a range of well known habitats. Certain animals and plants will make their home in a particular habitat.

Sandy beaches

With little stable ground in which plants can take root, beach animals resort to eating organic debris that is washed in on the tides.

Rocky coasts

Littered with boulders and pounded by waves, only the hardiest of plants and animals can survive and thrive on rocky shores.

Muddy coasts

The calm water and fine sediment of mangrove forests, tidal flats and salt marshes support plant life, which attracts animal life.

Ancient crab

Horseshoe crabs are not true crabs as their name suggests, but are closely related to spiders, ticks and scorpions. Horseshoe crabs are primitive animals that have existed in their present form for over 360 million years. They live in deep water, but come ashore once a year to mate.

On the cliffs

Puffins spend most of their lives at sea, but in the spring they return to the cliffs where they hatched. Here they form colonies of up to one million nests. Pairs of puffins will nest between rocks and under boulders. If there is soil they will make a nesting burrow or move into an empty rabbit burrow.

Atlantic horseshoe crabs on the shore

Atlantic puffins on a rocky cliff

Ocean forests

In the oceans and seas there are forests and **meadows** of seaweeds and **seagrasses**. Just like forests on land, these unusual **ecosystems** are bursting with life as they provide food and shelter for many species of animals. These watery **forests** and meadows help protect **coastlines** by absorbing the wave energy caused by **cyclones** and storms. In addition, these ecosystems are highly efficient at extracting **damaging** carbon dioxide out of the **environment**, meaning that they play an important role in combating **global** warming.

Seagrasses and seaweeds provide hiding places, breeding grounds and protective nurseries.

A large Pacific sea nettle jellyfish at the edge of a Californian kelp forest, USA.

Seagrass origins

Unlike seaweeds that originated in the oceans, seagrasses came from flowering plants that grew on dry land.

A useful plant

Kelp are large seaweeds. They are used in the manufacture of toothpastes, shampoos, salad dressings, puddings and cakes, dairy products, frozen foods, medicines and more!

Did you know?

Sea otters find their favourite food, sea urchins, in and around kelp forests. The otters wrap kelp stems around their bodies to stop them drifting away on the current while resting and eating.

Gassy floats

Like plants on dry land, kelp grows by using the Sun, through the process of photosynthesis, to produce energy. Kelp plants have floats, called bladders, which are small gas-filled balloons at the base of their blades. The bladders help the blades float so that they can absorb maximum sunlight.

Air bladders on a giant kelp plant

An octopus hunting in a seagrass meadow

Purple sea urchins eating seaweed

Grassy meadows

Seagrasses are found in tropical and colder regions. Like grasses on land, they form large meadows, produce flowers and seeds and are home to a diverse number of organisms. One seagrass plant can give rise to many stems, which are all connected by underground roots, over a wide area.

Hungry urchins

Sea urchins are the number one enemy of seaweed forests. These tiny, colourful creatures feed on the shoots and leaves of the plant and can demolish large areas of these underwater habitats. Starfish, ocean catfish and otters eat sea urchins and in doing so help to control urchin numbers.

Factfile

Life in the forests

Underwater seaweed forests shelter thousands of animal species including crabs, shrimps, brittle stars and sea cucumbers.

Sea lion
There is plentiful fish in the forests for the agile sea lion. It can dart and turn quickly through and around the waving fronds.

Garibaldi
The bright orange garibaldi is often found around the forest floor. It grows up to 38 centimetres long and can live for over 12 years.

Leopard shark
The body patterns on this shark help camouflage it in the dappled light that flickers through the seaweed forest.

Coral reefs

Coral reefs are underwater structures made of the **skeletons** of coral, which are marine invertebrate **animals**. These reefs are found in warm, shallow waters around the **Equator**. Reefs are the **oldest** ecosystems and support more species per metre than any other environment. They protect **coastlines** against wave damage caused by **cyclones** and storms. They provide the sand on beautiful coral beaches. Reefs are feeding, **spawning** and nursery **habitats** for many ocean creatures, and provide food and livelihoods for around one **billion** people worldwide.

Facts and figures

Largest barrier reef
The Great Barrier Reef, off the Australian coast, stretches for 2,300 kilometres.

Most diverse reef
The Coral Triangle is a huge expanse of reefs lying in waters between Indonesia, Malaysia Papua New Guinea, Philippines, Solomon Islands and Timor. It contains 75 per cent of all known coral species and 3,000 fish species.

Fastest-growing coral
Staghorn corals can grow 15 centimetres a year.

Rarest coral
Thought extinct since the 1890s, a colony of elkhorn coral has been found off the Marshall Islands in the north Pacific Ocean.

Oldest coral colony
A black coral, collected off Hawaii, has being carbon dated as being 4,265 years old.

Coral gets its colours from the tiny algae that live in it

Reefs are home to 15 per cent of known fish species, but cover less than one per cent of the world.

Did you know?

A coral polyp is only 1-3 millimetres across and grows 10 millimetres a year. Polyps can colonise huge tracts of seabed, but it takes around 300,000 years for a reef to form.

New species

Scientists and researchers believe that there are still millions of new species to be discovered living on the world's coral reefs.

Under threat

One-fifth of the planet's reefs are so seriously damaged they are beyond recovery. Of the remaining reefs, about half could die unless coral starts to regrow.

Hard coral: three-metre table corals

Soft coral: red sea fan moving in the current

Factfile

Reef fish

The reefs are home to about 4,000 species of fish. These fish are among the most colourful and beautifully patterned of any creature in the oceans.

Emperor angelfish

The dark stripe across its eyes is meant to confuse predators – they are unable to tell if the angelfish is approaching.

Clown triggerfish

To avoid being preyed on, this fish can extend its fins to lock itself into crevices. It uncovers its own food by squirting water at it.

Mandarinfish

Named for its colouring that resembles the robes of a Chinese mandarin, its skin releases toxins to warn predators to back off.

Hard and soft

There are 800 species of hard coral. The polyps have clusters of six tentacles. Algae in the polyp's tissue provides the materials to make the hard calcium carbonate skeleton. Soft coral polyps have eight tentacles and most have no hard 'skeleton'. They move in the current and have a jelly-like feel.

Giant clam

Giant clams fix themselves to coral reefs and stay their for their whole lives. They are the largest molluscs on Earth and achieve their enormous size by consuming the sugars and proteins produced by the billions of algae that live in their tissues.

The giant clam, like coral, relies on algae

Cleaner shrimp

Cleaner shrimps are found on many coral reefs. They benefit from a symbiotic relationship. In return for cleaning larger sea creatures, the shrimp gets its fill of nutritious parasites from the host's body. Up to 25 shrimps will congregate at 'cleaning stations' and do a dance to attract a host.

Pacific cleaner shrimp at work

Other Plant-like animals

When it comes to **peculiar** animals, these are perhaps the **oddest** of all. The green sea slug is an animal that behaves like a plant, while the sea anemone looks like a **flower** but is, in fact, a predatory animal. In the main, these **mostly** immobile animals are **filter** feeders that strain plankton and algae from the water. Though all are found in shallow **tropical** water – often coral reefs – some are at home in cold water at great **depths**. These plant-like animals are found **attached** to rocks or wrecks and sometimes **embedded** in sand, living alone or in communities.

Facts and figures

Longest-lived sponge
Giant barrel sponges found in the Caribbean are 2,300 years old.

Coral that's not
Fire coral is not a true coral, but a relative of sea anemones. Divers have suffered intense pain for two weeks after mistakenly touching it.

Medical uses
Many of these plant-like animals produce substances that have anti-cancer properties.

Largest sea anemone
Merten's carpet sea anemone can measure 1.5 metres in diameter. The smallest are just a few millimetres in size.

Chemical warfare
To get their share of space on crowded reefs, sponges release toxins that stop predators like sea squirts moving in.

Sea squirt sizes
The 3,000 species of sea squirt vary in size from 3–30 centimetres.

Some of the **largest sponges** may be **over 100 years old.**

Small fish and many invertebrates live on and in this huge barrel sponge

Easy being green

The green sea slug is able to extract photosynthesising genes from the algae it eats. The slug then uses this to make chlorophyll, in the same way as a plant!

Snail fur

Snail fur is a tiny plant-like animal that colonises the shell of a hermit crab. If its head is cut off, snail fur will grow another in a few days.

Did you know?

Sea squirts are a favoured food in South Korea, where they are known as sea pineapples. They are often eaten raw or pickled. Sea squirts are also food for colourful sea slugs!

A clever fish

Frogfish, or anglerfish, are irregularly shaped with bumpy, scale-less skin that is coloured to perfectly mimic sponges, like the purple tube sponge. Frogfish hide among the sponges to avoid getting eaten, while at the same time waiting for their own unsuspecting prey to approach.

Living together

Anemonefish are immune to anemone toxin, so hide in the anemone's tentacles and graze on leftover food. In return, the anemonefish shoos away predators and removes parasites. Anemones will sometimes attach themselves to hermit crabs – the camouflage protects the crab.

A frogfish hides among tube sponges

Some anemonefish and their host

Venus flower glass sponges with a squat lobster in the middle

Filter feeders

These animals filter their food – bacteria, plankton and small animals – from the water. Glass sponges are filter feeders. Silica needles fuse together to make their net-like skeletons and when water passes through the net, food is extracted. The net will also trap small animals.

Icy waters

The Southern and Arctic oceans are **different** to other oceans on Earth. They are **colder**, so the water is denser and sea ice and icebergs increase the **saltiness** of the water. As the denser water sinks, surface water is pulled in, creating huge **circulating** currents **thousands** of metres below the oceans' surface. The **Southern** Ocean surrounds the Antarctic land mass, while the **Arctic** Ocean has no land masses at all. Scientists believe that polar marine creatures have fewer offspring, live **longer** and grow larger, though more **slowly** than their warmer-water relatives.

Facts and figures

Fastest penguin swim
Gentoo penguins have been timed at 36 kilometres per hour!

Largest penguin colony
Two million chinstrap penguins gather to breed on Zavodovski Island, in the southern Atlantic Ocean.

Longest migration
Adélie penguins cover 13,000 kilometres a year between summer breeding sites and their winter hunting grounds.

Biggest seal
The record is held by a southern elephant bull seal that weighed 5,000 kilograms and measured 6.85 metres.

Most numerous
There are almost 12 million mating pairs of macaroni penguins in the world. This is a penguin record!

Fiercest polar animals
The polar bear and the Greenland shark share this honour.

Did you know?

Krill, a shrimp-like crustacean, is the favourite food of the planet's largest animal, the blue whale. Krill eat the phytoplankton that thrive in the Southern Ocean.

A polar bear swimming in the icy water of the Arctic ocean

Giant shark

The Greenland shark, found in waters 600 metres deep under the Arctic ice, can grow to eight metres and can kill a polar bear, though its normal diet is seal.

Polar dip

The polar bear paddles with its front paws and steers with its hind paws. It has a layer of warming blubber and its nostrils close underwater.

Polar bears can swim for days at a time and cover hundreds of kilometres.

A herd of walruses resting on the Arctic sea ice

Southern penguins

These flightless birds spend most of their life in water. They catch krill, fish and squid in their beaks and swallow them whole.

Chinstrap penguin

Found on the Antarctic Peninsula and islands of the South Atlantic, its colonies can consist of 100,000 breeding pairs.

Mighty walrus

A walrus spends a third of its life on sea ice and prefers snow-covered moving pack ice or ice flows to land. A layer of blubber, up to 15 centimetres thick, keeps it warm. It eats tubeworms, corals, crabs, shrimps, bivalve molluscs, seals and even other walruses. Killer whales and humans are its predators.

A weddell seal below a breathing hole in the Antarctic ocean

Adélie penguin

It spends summer on the Antarctic coasts. In winter it lives on pack ice that is thousands of kilometres from its summer home.

A perfect home

Some species of seal depend on sea ice to survive. It provides them with a frozen shelter in which to raise their cubs. Some seals use their teeth to keep natural holes in the ice open. They will use these 'breathing holes' to enter and exit the water while hunting and to escape predators.

'Spyhopping'

Spyhopping is a special behaviour among whales and dolphins. They leap from the water, then bob about with their heads above the water so they can have a look around. To hold this position, they kick their tail flukes. It is similar to humans treading water.

Arctic killer whales 'spyhopping'

King penguin

Found on many islands in the Southern Ocean, it never ventures onto pack ice. It incubates its egg on the top of its feet.

Giants of the ocean

Whales are warm-blooded **mammals** that can be found in all oceans, but each species will have its own **range** and migration routes. Whales are intelligent, **social** animals that nurture their young and **communicate** using movement, clicks and songs. They live together in **pods** of between two and 40 whales. Except for blue and grey whales, which are **solitary**. Whales have shown that, **within** the pod, they cooperate, plan, teach and even **grieve**. A lot is known about these magnificent animals, but there is much, much more to discover and **understand**.

Facts and figures

Largest whale
The record is held by a blue whale that measured 33 metres. Its heart was the size of a small car.

Longest lifespan
The bowhead whale is thought to be one of Earth's longest living animals, with a lifespan of 177–245 years.

Deepest diver
Cuvier's beaked whale can dive to depths of 2,992 metres.

Longest migration
A female humpback travelled 9,800 kilometres from Brazil in South America to Madagascar, off the east coast of Africa.

Most endangered
Northern right whales and blue whales are endangered. The north Pacfic northern right whale is nearly extinct.

Smallest whale
The dwarf sperm whale measures three metres.

Humpback whales travel in pods of up to 15 members

Did you know?

Some whales have teeth, others have baleen plates, that are covered with hairs that filter food from the water. The blue, fin and humpback are examples of baleen whales.

Long distance

The grey whale can travel 20,000 kilometres in its migration from summer feeding waters to winter breeding grounds.

Top of the chain

Whales are at the apex of the food chain, meaning they have few predators. But these giants are in trouble, with seven of the 13 great whale species regarded as vulnerable or endangered.

A humpback leaping clear of the water

A big leap!

Humpback whales are not only famous for their extra-long flippers, humped back and mating songs, but also for their athleticism. They can use their flippers and tail to propel them clear of the water! That takes some power when you consider they can weigh more than 40 small cars!

Mother and calf

After a long gestation, mother and calf form a strong bond, often staying virtually side by side – and even resting on its mother's head – for the first six months. After that the young calf will go on short forays alone, but will continue to feed on its mother's milk for a year or more.

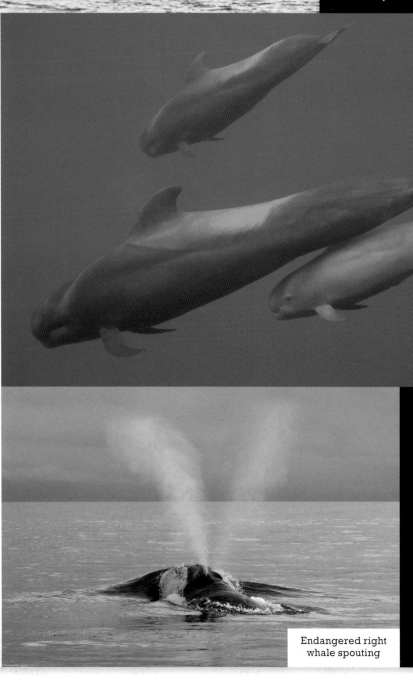
A female pilot whale with calves

Whale song

Humpback whales communicate, especially when migrating or mating, by singing. The songs may last for 30 minutes.

Clever!

A whale navigates using echolocation. Tissues in the whale's head process a reflected sound (an echo) so it can map its surroundings.

The blue whale is the loudest animal on Earth. Its call measures 188 decibels; louder than a jet engine!

Endangered right whale spouting

There she blows!

Baleen whales have two blowholes; toothed whales one. Whales can dive to great depths, but have to come to the surface to breathe. Blowholes, which are sealed under water, open at the surface to exhale air and mucus and to inhale fresh air. A vapour spout can reach nine metres into the air.

Fish

Marine **ecosystems** and the fish that inhabit them have a very **complex** relationship and one that is jeopardised by commercial fishing, pollution and a changing environment. The **diversity** of fish is **astounding** – from tiny, colourful fish that dart in and out of corals to deep-sea **monsters**, such as the Atlantic wolffish; from timid angelfish to **sleek** hunting machines, such as sharks and marlin. Although **different** from each other, they are all closely **connected** by the marine food chain, with even fish excreta being recycled as a **fertiliser** for algae and seagrasses.

Facts and figures

Top predator
The great white shark is the prime predator of marine fish and birds. It is also responsible for most attacks on humans.

Fastest swimmer
The sailfish can swim short distances at 109 kilometres per hour.

Largest school
It has been estimated that North Atlantic herring schools contain about three billion fish!

Most toxic fish to eat
The pufferfish is served as the delicacy fugu in restaurants in Japan. If it is not correctly prepared its toxin, which is 1,200 times stronger than cyanide, can be lethal.

Deepest, darkest home
The hadal snailfish has been recorded living in water down to a depth of 7.7 kilometres – where the water is near-freezing and it is completely dark!

Bony fish

The red lionfish (right) clearly shows the bony spines that connect the fins to body. The showy fins are venomous and can easily puncture skin. When disturbed, it flares its fins before attacking.

A red lionfish swimming over a coral reef in the Red Sea, Egypt

Over fishing

In 2012, commercial fishing extracted 90 million tonnes of fish from the seas. Overfishing is a global problem.

Did you know?

The ocean sunfish is the heaviest bony fish in the world, weighing in at 1,000 kilograms. It has a fish's head and tail with no body in the middle. It eats an awful lot of jellyfish!

After a 10-year study, scientists reported that there are 16,764 species of marine fish.

An anchovy with mouth and gills open

Breathing in water

Fish breathe oxygen that is dissolved in the water. As fish swim, water enters the open mouth and flows over layers of feathery gills in the throat. In the gills, oxygen is extracted from the water and enters the fish's bloodstream. The gills pass carbon dioxide from the bloodstream into the water.

Fatal stings

Ugly and dangerous are two words for the stonefish. Its dorsal spines can deliver fatal stings to humans. Camouflaged to look like an encrusted rock or piece of coral, the stonefish lies completely still until its prey swims by. It then takes and consumes its meal with amazing speed.

A deadly stonefish lies in wait

Giant fish

The manta ray can grow to eight metres with fins measuring seven metres, tip to tip. It is a giant fish, but it is dwarfed by the whale shark, coming in at around 12–14 metres. Though large, both of these fish feed on plankton. To filter as much water as possible, their mouths open very wide.

Manta ray: mouth open and feeding

Factfile

Types of fish

Fish make up the largest group of vertebrates – animals with a backbone and spinal column. There are four main types of fish.

Jawless fish

Lampreys and hagfish are fish without jaws. Their smooth, eel-shaped bodies have no scales.

Fish with cartilage

This includes sharks, rays, skates and chimaeras that all have skeletons made of cartilage, not bone.

Lobe-finned fish

These ancient fish have limb-like fins that move in an alternating pattern, like the legs of a trotting horse.

Ray-finned fish

This is the largest group, incorporating all bony fish that have fins attached to the body with bony spines.

Sharks

There are more than **465** species of shark, but only a handful of them have become **infamous**. There are eight categories of shark: flattened **angel** sharks, saw sharks, dogfish sharks, large-jawed mackerel sharks, placid carpet sharks, **bullhead** sharks, frilled and cow sharks, and **ground** sharks, which include some of the most **feared** hunters. Sharks live in all oceans around the world, and some **roam** far and wide. Most sharks produce only a few young, but within hours of being born, the **pups**, which have a full set of **teeth**, swim off and are ready to feed and fend for themselves.

Facts and figures

Smallest shark
At just 15 centimetres, you could hold the dwarf lantern shark in your hands. Rarely seen, it lives at depths below 250 metres.

How many teeth?
Over the course of its life, a shark could grow over 20,000 teeth.

Fastest sharks
It is a tie between mako sharks and blue sharks: both can swim at up to 97 kilometres per hour.

Long-range hunter
A great white shark was recorded swimming 20,000 kilometres between South Africa and Australia.

Fresh and salt water
The bull shark can tolerate both fresh and salt water. It has been found 4,000 kilometres up the Amazon River in South America.

Largest shark
The docile whale shark can grow to 13.5 metres.

Caribbean reef sharks have a torpedo-like body, flexible skeleton and excellent senses

Great whites can detect a drop of blood from over one kilometre away!

Did you know?

With the hammerhead shark's eyes at either end of its hammer-shaped head, this shark has outstanding binocular vision and an ability to see through 360 degrees.

Human threat

Sport and commercial fishing, accidental netting, poaching and pollution make humans a shark's number one predator.

Supreme carnivores

Hunting sharks pursue dolphins, fish, squid, seals and turtles. Cruisers swim open-mouthed, eating whatever enters. The bottom dwellers live on crabs, clams and molluscs.

Needle-sharp teeth of a sand tiger shark

Teeth for tearing

A hunting shark's large working teeth are at the front with rows of increasingly smaller teeth set behind. New teeth are always being grown to replace those lost. Sharks don't chew, but tear their prey and swallow great chunks. The teeth are set in skin, not bone, so teeth can move to fill a gap.

Feeding frenzy

Sharks like to dine alone, and when a number of sharks fight over the same prey a real frenzy can ensue. Sharks mass around the prey, thrashing and biting anything within reach – a behaviour seen in other animals. It is thought a frenzy occurs when prey sends out distress signals.

Factfile

An apex predator

Sharks top the food chain since they have no predators in their ecosystem. They keep in check the population of animals lower in the chain.

Great white shark

Built for speed and armed for hunting (it has 300 teeth), it is intelligent, has highly developed senses and can live for 60 years.

Tiger shark

Found in warm, shallow coastal waters, this shark will eat anything including sea snakes, stingrays and rubbish – even car tyres!

A school of lemon sharks in a feeding frenzy

Mega feeders

Megamouths, basking sharks and manta rays are filter feeders. A basking shark can draw up to 2,000 tonnes of water an hour into its mouth. The water is expelled through the gills, leaving food trapped on the denticles. The megamouth has tiny light-emitting organs around its mouth to attract small fish.

A megamouth, in full feeding mode

Bull shark

This is one of the most dangerous sharks. It is very strong, territorial and unpredictable. It bumps its prey – and then eats it.

Crustaceans

Crustacea is a difficult group to **define** because it is a diverse collection of 30,000 to 45,000 species. Crustaceans **dominate** water in the same way that **insects** dominate land, although some live on land too. Some crustaceans spend their lives **fixed** to objects, some move about **freely**. The hermit and mangrove crabs, for example, can **climb** trees! Crustaceans can't even agree on how to eat. There are **hunters**, filter feeders, scavengers and parasites. Their size varies enormously, too. They can be so **tiny** they live between grains of sand – or **giant** like the Japanese spider crab.

Facts and figures

Largest barnacle
The giant barnacle, which is found off the coasts of Spain and Chile, grows to 30 centimetres in height.

Biggest crab
The Japanese spider crab measures 3.8 metres across.

Deep-sea crustacean
The tiny, prawn-like *Hirondellea gigas*, lives in the Marianas Trench – 11 kilometres under the Pacific Ocean.

Smallest crab
The male pea crab measures one centimetre across.

Heavyweight
At 22 kilograms, the blue-green-brown American lobster is the heaviest crustacean.

Run away!
When a shrimp moves forward, it walks. But for rapid escapes, it swims backwards by curling and uncurling its abdomen.

Did you know?

The sea slater is a crustacean and is found wherever there is water. Tiny and abundant, it is critical in food chains. Some make their home on host fish as parasites.

The aggressive peacock mantis shrimp strikes its prey with force (100 times its own weight) and speed (120 kph)

Hermit crab

The hermit crab is not a true crab. It has a soft underbody that it protects by making its home inside a discarded shell. As it grows, it moves into larger shells.

Pistol shrimp

One snap of the pistol shrimp's giant claw can kill its prey. It lives in colonies with a queen and worker shrimps.

As a crustacean grows, it sheds its exoskeleton to accomodate its expanding body!

To cut or crush?

The pincers, or claws, of a common lobster are different sizes. The smaller claw has sharper edges and is for cutting. The larger is used for crushing prey. A fan-like tail helps it balance. It can grow to a metre in length, weigh up to five kilograms, and it can walk as well as swim.

Hungry crabs

Crabs primarily eat algae, but will also feed on molluscs, worms, bacteria, other crustaceans, and leftovers. It appears that the largest crabs are those that consume plants and animals. The chewing part of eating happens inside the stomach, which is lined with ridges for grinding the food down.

Common lobster: formidable pincers

A red rock crab scavenging on a rope

Feathery plume

The gooseneck barnacle is a filter-feeder. It has feathery tentacles that emerge from the shell to strain food out of flowing water. Highly prized as a food, gathering the barnacle takes daring. It attaches itself to rocks and other objects by a long stalk, thriving on shores that are pounded by waves.

Feathery gooseneck barnacle tentacles

Factfile

Crustacean groups

Some crustaceans are commercially valuable, and as such their stocks can be dangerously reduced by overfishing.

Krill
In the Southern Ocean their mass is 417 million tonnes, which is more than Earth's human mass. Krill eat plankton.

Barnacles
These filter-feeders live on any hard surface, even shelled animals. Once 'glued' to a home, they build a shell for life.

Crab, shrimp and lobster
These have a hard exoskeleton of chitin and calcium. Their multiple limbs can spear, crush or catch prey.

Echinoderms

Sea urchins, starfish and **crown** of thorns are among the most well known echinoderms. They are present in all **oceans** at every depth, even in the dark **abyss** (deep sea) zone. These unusual animals have a **hydraulic** network of canals in their bodies that power tiny tube feet. All enchinoderms have radial **symmetry**. This is easiest to spot in **starfish** as their arms extend outwards from the centre of their bodies in a symmetrical **pattern**. These incredible animals are able to **regenerate** missing limbs, arms, spines – even **intestines**!

Starfish range in diameter from two centimetres to 1.2 metres!

The Egyptian starfish has a protective, bony skin and can regenerate itself using part of a severed limb

Did you know?

A starfish eats a sea urchin by wrapping itself around the urchin and pushing its stomach out through its mouth. Acids dissolve the spines and shell, leaving the meat to be eaten.

Scare tactics

To alarm a predator, a sea cucumber can force its organs out through its body. Luckily, it can regrow these organs.

Sea hedgehog

Sea urchins were once called sea hedgehogs. It is easy to see the spiny similarity between urchins and hedgehogs. Long ago, in old English, urchin was the name for a hedgehog!

Tube feet

An echinoderm moves around (or sticks fast) thanks to its 'feet' – thousands of tiny tubes on the animal's underside. Water is forced from sacs into the tubes to make the sucker-like feet extend or contract. The tubes also allow the animal to feed and breathe. An adult sunflower starfish has about 15,000 tube feet.

Hollow tubes end in sucker-like feet

A five-limbed red cushion starfish

A seventeen-limbed crown of thorns starfish

Natural symmetry

All echinoderms have radial symmetry, often based on the number five. This means that lines of even length can be drawn from the limbs to one central point. These animals have no left or right, only an upper side and an underside. This symmetry means than every facet of an immobile echinoderm can defend and gather food.

Hidden mouths

A sea urchin's mouth is on the urchin's underside and is surrounded by protective spines that trap food. Its mouth, like that of a starfish, has five feeding plates. The mouth of the sea cucumber is surrounded by feeding tentacles that can be retracted.

Five feeding plates in a sea urchin's mouth

Seabirds

Seabirds spend so much time away from **land**, it is difficult to comprehend their lives on the **wing**. They fly astounding **distances**, often through near-gale force winds over angry oceans, dropping from the sky to **snatch** a fish. And all to be able to **nest** on a tiny outcrop of rock. Then, after dedicating months to raising their **young**, they set off for the hazardous return journey. Seabirds, like many other animals, are **threatened** by invasive predators at nesting sites, rubbish and **pollution** in the oceans and accidental longlining by **commercial** fishing fleets.

Facts and figures

Super migrator
Arctic terns live for up to 30 years and travel more than two million kilometres (equal to three round trips to the Moon) in their lifetime.

Sun filters
The retinas of a seabird's eyes contain a red-coloured oil that cuts the glare reflected off sand and water.

Smallest seabird
The storm petrel is a tiny 13–26 centimetres.

Deep diver
The emperor penguin can dive 565 metres and stay under water for 20 minutes.

Largest wing span
That belongs to the wandering albatross – at a massive 3.5 metres.

In danger
Of 346 seabird species 97 are threatened, with the albatross a big concern. Nearly half of all seabird species have declining populations.

Dull but clever
A seabird's light-coloured underside is hard to spot against the sky; the dull upper side veils it against the water below.

A diving gannet, with a fish firmly grasped in its beak, breaks through the water's surface

Wing shape
To aid long-distance flying, some seabirds have long, tapered wings. This improves a bird's ability to soar on currents, saving energy. Diving birds have shorter wings.

Burrow-nesting petrels use smell to navigate to their musky nesting burrows.

Did you know?
The wandering albatross can live for over 40 years, spending 85 per cent of those years at sea. It can travel 16,000 kilometres in a single journey and circle the globe in 46 days!

Webbed feet

Webbed feet help seabirds to paddle efficiently and propel them across the water fast enough to get lift-off. The addition of claws on webbed feet makes fishing easier. Blue feet (see right) don't help boobies swim, but will give a male a better chance of courting a female than a male with dull feet.

No mistaking blue-footed boobies

Bass Island, Scotland hosting gannets

Back on land

Each summer, hundreds of thousands of seabirds squeeze onto rocky outcrops, small islands and cliffs in order to nest. There is safety in numbers – predators find it hard to pick out a victim when the birds are packed tightly together. It is important since seabirds often only lay one egg.

Salty water

If you spend your life in, on, under or over seawater you are going to take in a lot of salt when you eat or drink. An excess would cause dehydration, which is why most seabirds have a gland that extracts the salt from their food and water. It is discharged from their nostrils.

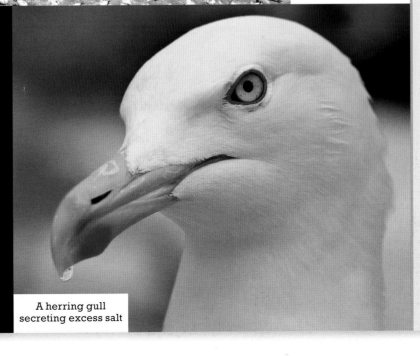

A herring gull secreting excess salt

Factfile

Feeding strategies

How a seabird gets its food is down to how it has evolved and adapted, its specific habitat and how it functions.

Surface feeders
A frigatebird dips its beak just under the surface of the water and picks up its prey mid-flight.

Pursuit diver
A penguin dives underwater and propels itself with its wings or feet. It will chase its prey.

Plunge diver
By diving from a height while in flight, the pelican can go 70 metres under water to get food.

Scavenger
The skua raids nests for eggs and chicks, snatches food from another's claws or eats dead animals.

Glossary

Algae
A single or multi-celled organism that has no roots, stems or leaves and is often found in water.

Apex predator
An animal who has no natural predators in its ecosystem. Apex predators sit at the top of the food chains. Apex predators include whale sharks, bull sharks, killer whales, humpback whales and polar bears.

Bacteria
Microscopic living organisms, usually one-celled, that can be found everywhere.

Camouflage
Colours, patterns and shapes that make an animal difficult to see against its background.

Consumers
All animals are consumers. They are unable to make their own food, so they need to consume plants and/or animals to obtain energy.

Crustacean
An animal, such as a crab or lobster, that has a hard covering, or exoskeleton, and two pairs of antennas, or feelers.

Currents
A continuous flow of water in the ocean. Some currents are surface currents while other currents are much deeper, flowing hundreds metres below the water's surface.

Decomposers
An organism, such as a bacteria or fungus, that consumes dead organisms and returns them to ecological cycles.

Denticle
A small tooth or tooth-like projection.

Echinoderm
Marine invertebrates with tube feet and radially symmetrical bodies, such as starfish, sea urchins and sea cucumbers.

Echolocation
A method of sensing nearby objects by using pulses of high-frequency sound. Echoes bounce back from obstacles and other animals.

Ecosystem
A community of plants or animals and the environment to which they are adapted.

Equator
An imaginary line around Earth, which separates the Northern and Southern hemispheres.

Exoskeleton
An external skeleton that supports and protects an animal's body. Some exoskeletons cannot grow, so have to be shed and replaced at times during the animals life.

Filter feeders
An animal that collects food by straining small prey from seawater.

Food chain
A a community of organisms in which one forms food for another, which in turn is eaten by another, and so on.

Fungi
Organisms, such as mushrooms and moulds, that contain no chlorophyll and that live parasitically on living and dead organisms.

Gills
Organs that collect oxygen from water and are used for breathing.

Glacier
A huge mass of ice formed from snow falling and accumulating over years.

Isopod
A crustacean with seven pairs of legs adapted for crawling.

Molluscs
An animal, such as a snail or squid, with no backbone and a soft body that is often partly, or fully covered by a shell.

Overfishing
The practice of fishing so much that the fish are unable to sustain their population. The fish get fewer and fewer, until eventually there are none left to catch.

Photosynthesis
A chemical process that allows organisms to capture energy in sunlight and convert it into food.

Phytoplankton
Microscopic plants that live in the ocean and form the plant components of plankton.

Plankton
Small plant and animal organisms that float or drift in great numbers in fresh or salt water. It is the first link in the marine food chain and is eaten by many organisms, including mussels, fish, birds, and some marine mammals.

Producers
Organisms that produce their own food. They do this by converting light energy from the Sun.

Radial symmetry
A form of symmetry in which the body is shaped like a wheel, often with the mouth in the centre.

Tornado
A funnel of spinning air that forms beneath a thundercloud.

Toxins
A poison produced by certain animals, plants, or bacteria.

Waves
Waves are disturbances in the ocean that transmit energy from one place to another. Waves are usually created by wind on the ocean's surface.

Zooplankton
The tiny animal parts of plankton. Zooplankton is mainly made up of small crustaceans and the larvae of fish.

Index